Graciously

Dr. Rosemari Grigsby

Acknowledgment

I acknowledge the Holy Spirit who has guided me. I acknowledge Jesus Christ, who is my salvation and through whom I have been redeemed. I acknowledge God the Father Yehoshua, the 'I am' the 'Alpha and Omega' who lives within me.

I thank God for acknowledging the many praises I send up daily, and I claim the many blessings the Heavenly Host has in store for me.

I acknowledge the mustard seed of faith that ripples like a wave in a pond and grows until it reaches the shore.

I acknowledge my journey into your heart by way of the words given to me from my Father.

May He bless you as he has me.

Contenido

Acknowledgment 2

Introduction 1

Chapter One 4

    Grace 5

    I Am 8

    The Light 11

    Man Unlimited 14

    Feeling You 18

    Time 21

Chapter Two 24

    You Said 25

    The Spirit Of Love 28

    Fix It 30

    Today 32

    Cries for Freedom 35

    Wings 38

    Save Me 41

Chapter Three 42

    Favor 43

    The Way 45

    The Prize 47

Love in Truth 51

The Power Within 54

I know He Hears Me 56

Chapter Four *58*

The Masterpiece 59

This Title 61

Honey 64

So I Wait 67

Life 73

Chapter Five *76*

Come In.. 77

My Peace 80

Here and There I Am 82

Let Me In.. 86

Thank You 90

Not mine.. 91

The one became two 93

Chapter Six *97*

Abba 98

Distress.. 100

Ask Yourself 102

Everyday 105

In My Head 107

Sedative.. 109

Remember 111

Love covers all 112

Introduction

In life, we journey through many passages filled with trials and tribulations, but there is always light at the end of the tunnel. We only need to reach out, open our hearts and minds to be receptive to the love and faith that lies within us.

Both love and pain are universal; therefore, both are felt by all.

We are all in the classroom of life where no one fails- we just take the test over-knowing that the love of God is the teacher, and through Grace, we will overcome.

Cada prosa de este libro se abre con una nueva experiencia y termina con un rayo de Esperanza. Cada prosa es un capítulo de una vida, una historia en sí misma, tal vez tu vida, tal vez tu historia.

Siéntate, lee y piensa en los muchos Ángeles que han tocado tu vida mediante una palabra o un acto en un momento de necesidad. Considera este pequeño libro y sabe que los mensajeros de Dios siempre están cerca.

Graciously

Chapter One

Grace

What is the space

between right and wrong

The time between day and night The

trail of life

from childhood to adulthood...

from failure to success

What is the place called

That gives us all

the chance to go on and keep

our heads high and hearts open,

That space allows for

forgiveness

When all is said and done.

Grace is this place,

this space in time

This refuge of God's invention

It's just there, by God

Grace is not earned or asked for,

from God to all

Grace is that space,

that time, that place

Grace is granted to all.

I Am

I am what I am by Grace

precious Grace of God

given as promised freely

not earned but paid for

by my Lord Jesus Christ

I am what I am given to be

I am what my Father wants

of me

To be led by Him

not of myself

I am but clay to be molded

A slave to His spirit but free

Grace, love, long-suffering

Jesus Christ, for me

I am unworthy

But made worthy by Grace.

Yehoshua's Tender Mercies

The Light

There is work to be done

by the chosen ones

sent down by the Light

Into the womb

Their journey began

Filled with holy insight.

The strife of Darkness

blows evil winds

sent to conquer the Light

But Light over Darkness

will always win

The Light is forever in sight.

Though pain & strife will

Follow the Light,

they will be overcome,

for Light is love, comfort

and truth

and through Light

All battles are won

Man Unlimited

The sky how high does it go

an eagle How high does it fly man

Limitless timeless spaceless for

the unlimited ways of his will who can

take back the gifts given to him in the

beginning

who can control the unlimited power

within

to speak any idea into reality

man made a little lower than Angels by

the power of God

man where is his heart his soul given to

him only to hold in this space

this place and time man,

mindful of an end thoughtless of when

his folly will reward him

man. This chance this time this place

let it be safe.

Graciously

love the key

can't you see

the power within yourself

to stay centered in the light

love is the only place of safety and

peace,

love planted in you

from the beginning

man you are forever, linked to the love

cord,

of your maker just reach out and touch

yourself

Graciously

the power of love,

your maker

All one

all in you

man your power

your love,

Unlimited, like your God unlimited

Man

Feeling You

I feel your courage,

I feel your pain

I see your tears,

forever in my mind

I feel so helpless,

With all this rain,

Will we ever see the sun again

In the middle of the night

I hear your cries

They awaken me

I feel so helpless, all this rain.

Angel of mercy shine

I feel so helpless; all this pain

Angel of mercy, please shine.

Warm us

with your inner peace,

love and strength

help us

To put it all together again.

Angel of mercy

Heal these hearts & minds

Angel of mercy, please shine

Time

Faith has but one time

NOW

time serves us

NOW

time was made for us

In the beginning

but it waits not for us

so we must use it wisely

and quickly

NOW

it is precious and irreplaceable

Graciously

our Maker has no beginning and no

love faith everlasting use the time

NOW

faith

knowing that all is possible

in time

Our Father's words will always come

to pass in

TIME

Chapter Two

You Said

You said, "long life salvation."

You said "cities of gold."

You said, "no pain or sorrow."

You said you would be there

to hold

Through you, I am free

Because you are in me,

My problems are yours

You are my strength,

All battles are won

Through you, I am free

Where ever I may be.

You said, "come all who labor."

You said, "find rest in me."

You said, "fear not; I am with you."

You said you are all I need

Jesus Christ, Lord & Savior

You said, "thine will be done."

The Spirit Of Love

Love ❤ The spirit or the gender

which do you see first?

True love lingers through time through

physical being through spiritual light!

Love is the endless answer the only key

to eternal happiness and peace.

No form or gender can stop the

overwhelming flow of true love.

Love conquers all Love touches all

Love heals all

Love saves all

Lust is never an issue for love has no

gender

Fix It

Sometimes we must look behind or

even go back

to button a hole or straighten a pleat,

to make our life tidy & neat

A forgotten chore,

or misplaced word

Left unattended could creep,

Along for years, they could grow,

and cause tears

We thought we would never weep.

Now sleeping is good,

but each night before slumber

Ask God to let us all see

The day we just passed

with compassion to last, until

the next day to repent & repeat

with kindness overlooked,

while waiting the chance to fix it

Or patch it real neat.

With Godly expression, love and

compassion then

That flaw we will never remeet

Today

Today I felt the wind

against my face

I smelled the air, its freshness

had been erased from my memory

The sunlight warm and bright

Hurt my eyes, a pleasant pain

I squinted it away, then smiled

Could it be over, the storm,

the rain, the real pain of my life

or just the light

at the end of the dark

another turn in the maze of life

this life given without request

this life !!!!! Am I really doing

my best

Father help me

to be free

Embrace my spirit

Transform my heart

Then stay with me

Cries for Freedom

My soul cries out

to be free

A prisoner, it is where

It does not want to be

It has no control

over the members of this vessel

It's trapped

and longs to be free

It cries out for help

to tame this beast of worldly

Greed it will not fall into

submission by its own

selfish need

My soul cries out

to do good and right

then that worldly beast

appears from out of sight

To steal and kill

the will of the righteous me

that my soul has vowed

to be

My Father will help

I only need to cry out

His name

So my soul cries out

Jesus

Wings

If I could grow wings

And fly away

I'd head straight up for the sky.

The warmth of the sun

the mystery of stars

I'd wave to the moon bye-bye.

If I could grow wings

I'd see wondrous things

all of God's creation

Formed from his love,

Just dust we were,

The seas, mountains, terrains.

If I could grow wings

I'd just visit this earth and

Heaven would be my home.

The freedom of wind,

the love of God, watching Him

sit on His throne,

Would keep me in awe

just long enough, then

I'd go to all others and sing,

Praises & glory, we've all heard

In stories and tell them it's True,

so marvelously true

It's there just as written

Just waiting for you.

Save Me

I cry to you, father help me to be free

embrace my spirit, transform my heart,

then stay with me

Chapter

Three

Favor

The favor of God rest upon you

He is here for you, he made you

And is waiting for you with arms wide

open.

He is not for you for what you are

going to be

Or what you were, His favorite is on

you for you.

He is a loving father, who is for you,

His favor, rest upon you,

His spirit lives within you he loves you,

Graciously

His favor rest upon you.

The Way

The way

What is

What was

What will be

Today

Tomorrow

Forever

The rock

Forever

The light

Jesus

The Prize

I started a journey in search of me

trying to be all

The world thought I should be

I tried and tried but

There was no end,

to filling the hole

The world put me in

Then finally, I knew

I'd never find me

I'd never give what the world

wanted from me

That thought

brought tears to my eyes

Then I began to realize that it

was OK to be lost,

in the most enlightened way.

Lost in His shadow,

lost in His love

Lost in the truth of what comes

From above.

God loves us and leads us

to see the flood of light

That gives love eternally.

Lost in His glory,

lost in His peace,

lost in Christ,

Who died for you and me.

So don't be deprived of this gift

given freely

No work is required

He loves us so dearly

Don't miss the Prize

due to worldly eyes

This gift is everlasting and yours

Just for asking

Love in Truth

I never knew what I could do

to touch you from afar

I never thought

The things I bought

would be forgotten relics,

of love misplaced

from a heart untaught

to look for love in truth

The love, in truth, I never knew

even though

I saw right through you

Your heart was shielded

By the patch, you thought

not we're taking out by a patch you

thought

would heal you and putting in by the

patch you thought

would heal you

Love, in truth, was out of sight

And I think you knew it

The light of day will send a ray

of power to heal

Then seal it

Just move the patch

And trust the light

Let love in truth prove it

The Power Within

A great windstorm arose
And beat my vessel so,
That it weakened to the point
of near destruction.

As the Holy Spirit slept
within my soul, waiting
to be summoned by my will
I cried out,
"Do you not care if we perish?"

A reply came, "Do you not care?"

Where is your faith?

Call on your power?

It's here within,

Rebuke the storm

And praise the Father,

Rise up in your faith,

Your power is within

Victory is in your hand.

I know He Hears Me

I know that he hears me

from the deepest cosmos in the universe

from my beginning that will end in his

arms

I know he feels

my joy

my pain

my confusion

and gives me

resolution for peace

and love

from above all around

never lost

always found sitting

in the mist of his love

being still and knowing that he is my

God for real and

I know he love's me

Chapter

Four

The Masterpiece

How is it that the stars appear

to lay upon my lawn,

glowing in the moonlight

on this crisp winter night

The trees dressed in wedding white

like a bride so elegantly

lit against the sky

The artist of this scene

must truly be a Master

who but a Master could conceive

such perfection with such ease,

this masterpiece that glows

upon the night

this masterpiece

that brings my eyes

such delight

This masterpiece

the artist, my Master, indeed

This Title

This title around my neck

a love affair gone sour

The more I strive, the

heavier the load of my labor gets

The web of duties given to me

performed once so lovingly

have burdened my mind,

body, and soul

Now it's love turned to hate

and I don't know how to escape

I've worked my lifetime to

stay afloat

but now I want to jump

off this boat

Look at that bird sitting in his nest

he does not labor, nor does he sow

he eats, sleeps, flies, and rests

Who provides him this luxury

must I put in a petition for him

to help me

His yoke is easy, so I have read

He calls all who labor to rest

In Him could it be, that He

will make a way for me

He will

It is written

Honey

Honey is what makes the bees

hum around the flower.

Honey is the sweetness

that causes man

to cross the seas in search of love

yes that sweetness of honey

Honey is the smooth,

gentleness felt

by the summer breeze in the trees

as the leaves float

down to the ground

a perfect landing with ease

Honey, the clouds many shapes

and sizes

just passing from land to sea

Honey, the sweet love

the golden glow

as light reflects its rays

Honey, God's natural glow

his love flowing

Honey is His touch His Spirit

His sweet love.

So I Wait

In my distress I seek serenity

but do not find it

In my distress I seek, I seek and

nothing is of comfort to me

for very long

In my distress I ask

for a shoulder, a hand, a sign

of some sort, to show

that I am not alone

In my distress

My lonely anguish of existing

while in search of inner peace

the purpose, the reason for me,

the map I must travel to be free,

to leave this frame of mind

my spirit seeks its maker,

my body seeks its likeness

In no man have I found rest

or an answer to end my quest

of longing for the warmth

of the nest that eagles fly to

high in the sky

The quest for the peace

of the flowers in spring,

the warm glow of the sun gently

caressing my face and

The winds sweet flow

against my entire being

bringing with it the fragrance

of Spring, Summer, Fall

or even Winter for they all know

their purpose here but me,

not a clue as to what I am to do

This is my distress

for I cannot elude to a safe place

I listen but do not hear

a voice to guide me

I cry out, but only

my echo returns

Perhaps I'm in the wrong place

the wrong time

perhaps I must wait

until redeemed by my maker

through a secret plan

So I Wait

I wait!

I wait

Life

Come dance with me or

I will pass you by

Come dance with me now

for I have no time to wait

Dance with me quickly

others want to drink of me

and be full

Dance with me, hurry

you have only one change

grab me before I pass you by

Come dance

my music is bitter sweet,

yes but the sweet seasons the bitter

to a blend of perfection

Dance, the band plays on

the tune is never ending

Take this dance, this chance

Come !!! Dance

the dance of life

Chapter Five

Come In

I am not tall and slender

I am not young and tender

Only my heart is tender,

but guarded

by the season of knowledge

I am not fashionable and polished

I am not a scholar

by man's standards

but I know the word of my Lord

I am not a trinket to be displayed

to play the games' of the world

by looking the part

of the in crowd'

But my gentle manner will appease

the storm of discontent

and calm the fury

of disappointing lies

told by worldly eyes

I am not one

who leads by force

or brute domination

I am not one

who lays down and plays dead

in the face of injustice

My eyes are open

my mind is open

my heart is open

Won't you come in!

My Peace

I send you my peace

I send past times

of happy me and happy you

I send, I send you

a little piece of me

For me to be there right now

cannot be, so

I send you my peace

Graciously

Your future might seem bleak now,

but close your eyes

daydream of what was

let yesterday take you through

today

and into tomorrow

I do only what I can do

and that is

to send you my peace

a beat from my heart

a breath from my body

and words from my soul

Here and There I Am

You see me in the trees

the leaves

green

yellow

red

and brown

and naked with no leaves at all

spring

winter

summer

fall

blessings to all

Graciously

Stardust kissed by the sun

warming your bodies

everyone

Father

Creator

Orchestrator

says

I see You

I hear You

I love You

I am The I Am

Look see I Aam

all around

Graciously

taste and see that

blessings for all

Sun-kissed stardust

warming up the bodies

all

Father

Creator

Orchestrator

says

I see you

I hear you

I love you

I am He I Am

Look see I am

around

Graciously

I Am good

it is me inside of you

my Beloved

Let Me In

Sent by my Father

to enter in this world of sadness

this world of sin

to do my part to bring an end

to suffering within

but this spirit can't find a home

a place to grow for very long

so much despair

within these vessels

they push me out, they cannot feel

they know not where

my journey began

I know not where it ends

I can't find a place to enter in

please stop one moment

to help a friend

who's here again please let me in

this one more birth might

put an end

might save a soul,

might lead it home

give me a chance

to sprout and bloom

a chance to end

my brother's gloom

a chance to do my Father's work

Please let me in I can't desert

the task I have been given

from God's light to daylight

God's love to you

Thank You

Jesus at my head post

Jesus at my feet

Jesus touch my hands,

my every need he meets

Jesus in the morning

Jesus night time too

Jesus feeds my body, mind,

and spirit too

Not mine

This body borrowed,

a temporary vessel

To be used And cared for until

my father calls me home

I have work

I have lessons

I have deeds for others,

all to be done

Graciously

as lead by my maker, my father

My Lord

this body,

no matter how big

or how small,

how twisted

or lacking limbs

is perfect to do his will

Remember

It is written

we are made in his image

Graciously

The one became two

wake up from the dream of another
place,

Another existence,

you are here now

by the will and grace of God, our
father,

except your assignment here

he made you in his image

Be true to your Fathers handy work

Be true to that image

God, our father, the one who truly
loves us GENDERS no matter.

The one became two

Maybe there was left some residue

But still the one became two

*You and I have a purpose designed for
an assignment*

*everyone has an assignment everyone
who is birthed*

*comes to this place ,With purpose that
only you could fulfill*

Everyone has an assignment we are
Uniquely designed for that assignment.

no blame no shame the one became two

fulfill your destiny Be blessed accepting

his love

Yes! YOU are his masterpiece

YES. The one became two!!

Jesus, thank you, Jesus

Jesus, thank you, Jesus

send up praise to you

is all I know to do

Call on you at noontime

morning, night time too

wash away my sad face

wash away my sins

open up my spirit let your glory in

Jesus, thank you, Jesus

Chapter

Six

Graciously

Abba

Gentle Strong

Inside And out

to know him

is to love him

To feel see

an overwhelming

Comfort and peace

To know him is to love him

Abba your maker

loved you First

With enough love to spread

like honey through out the whole

universe Love attracts good vibes let

that love shine through your eyes

 Distress

Talk it out

write it out

Let it out

let it go It's all his

let it go.

Overlook and make allowance for hasty
thoughtless words and deeds
love covers all

Know that the sun will shine

Let it brighten your day

Let the SON (word of God)

Graciously

Guild you day by day

Stay strong in the Lord

Love yourself

He made You in his image

He is the potter

we are the clay

Being molded by his hands

day by day

101

Ask Yourself

why are you not following his

instructions

Many have failed to tell others about

the Christ

and how he paid the ultimate price

are you seeing the tribulations that

are hitting All the nations

old time religion

what is your decision

our maker is coming back for a people

without spot or wrinkle

he cleaned. Us

die for us

claimed us

saved us

disasters earthquake

tornadoes

tragedies of all kinds

like the days of Noah we have been told

one thing is clearly true he is talking to

me and you

no matter what others may claim

God's words remains the same

let go of self

let his spirit flow

murió por nosotros

know that he is here and

Forever Alpha and Omega

We are being told so

why not listen!

Everyday

I think

every day could be your day to show

love and kindness

show love and care everywhere you

venture

yes every day and everywhere your

maker leads you

where ever you are lead wherever your

steps are ordered

tell everyone of your love

NOW

While you still can

and always reach out with a helping

hand mother father sister brother

stranger on the street

even greatly disadvantaged

one that you may meet

Then

think on this

But for the Grace of God

there go I

In My Head

In my head, a faceless figure in the

night invites its self to me, so naturally,

could it feel at home

in my space,

my aura,

my world,

this world,

that I conceal so securely

the graceful bows

the empty smiles

filled with stay away,

inviting a shadow of reality so

this figure cannot be

it's just a ghost of memories

lingering from the past

how long will they last?

my sleep, beckons it to my bed

my death will backing it to my grave

Unless I allow myself to be saved.

Sedative

I am your sedative

Take a piece of me

As you will

I am here for the taking

As time goes on

The cycle of past negativities

Can only be broken by you

I am only a sedative

Temporary Reliever

Not a real solution

I am really a lie

Truth wins

Jesus

the truth the way

The light

from the author......

Remember

We are all spirits who have a soul

we live in a body that may be

pressed down from time to time

but never forsaken

Some nights tears may fall

but always remember that

joy comes with the morning sun

just look to the light

and know you are loved

God's Grace be with you

Graciously

Love covers all

Overlook and make allowance for hasty

thoughtless words and deeds

love covers all

Know that the sun will shine
Let it brighten your day

Let the SON (word of God)
Guild you day by day

Stay strong in the Lord
Love yourself

Graciously

He made You in his image

He is the potter

we are the clay

Being molded by his hands

day by day

Love covers all!!!

www.ingramcontent.com/pod-product-compliance
Lightning Source LLC
Chambersburg PA
CBHW040150160726
48006CB00014B/1682